DEVON'S RAILWAYS

Helen Harris

Bossiney Books • Exeter

Above: points on the Haytor Granite Tramway, still visible today
Title page photograph: building the line between Hatherleigh and Halwill Junction; the line opened in 1925

Cover: climbing Goodrington Bank on the Paignton & Dartmouth Railway, August 1993

This reprint 2023 First published 2001
Bossiney Books Ltd, 68 Thorndale Courts, Whitycombe Way, Exeter, EX4 2NY
www.bossineybooks.com
ISBN 978-1-915664-08-2

Acknowledgements
The author gratefully acknowledges the help given by Mr S Church, Environment Department, Devon County Council, concerning recent developments on Devon railway lines; also the kindness of individuals and bodies in allowing access for photographic purposes.

The author and publishers are grateful to the following for permission to reproduce photographs: The Beaford Photographic Archive, pp 1, 11, 12, 18, 19, 22, 26, 28, 29, 34, 35, 36, 38 and 39; Bernard Mills, cover and pp 7, 17 and 44; B Mills Collection, pp 5, 6, 10, 14, 15, 31, 32, 33 and 40; Royal Institution of Cornwall, p 37.

The following photographs are by the author: pages 42, 45, 46 and 47.

Map by Robin Paris.

Printed in Great Britain by Booths Print, Penryn, Cornwall

Before the main lines

While railways in the generally accepted sense did not reach Devon until the 1840s, smaller systems, more properly termed tramways, had already been supporting local industries for several decades.

Simple tramways were used in mining, for carrying small trams or wagons which were either pushed by men or drawn by horses. At Wheal Friendship, Mary Tavy, where copper and lead were mined from the eighteenth century, an inclined shaft sunk around 1826 by the engineer John Taylor carried a 3 ft gauge tramway (powered by a 40 ft waterwheel) on which ore was brought to the surface in 20-25 cwt wagons.

Taylor was also engineer for the Tavistock Canal, opened in 1817, which carried ore from Tavistock to the River Tamar at Morwellham. The 237 ft descent from the canal to the riverside over an inclined plane carried a double set of iron rails fixed to stone sleepers; some of these, with drilled holes, can still be seen today. Cargoes were off-loaded from the canal boats on to small trucks bound for the quay, power being provided by a waterwheel that was sited at the top and had chain attachments.

Another canal which extended into Devon from Cornwall and used water-powered inclined planes was the Bude Canal, constructed between 1819 and 1825. In this case the boats (carrying their cargoes) were fitted with wheels and themselves travelled on the rails.

Tramways were also used to carry stone. In 1812 the 3 ft 6 in gauge Plymouth Breakwater Railway was laid from Plymouth's Oreston Quay to the nearby pier for carrying large stones to boats during the breakwater construction, under the engineer John Rennie.

A few years later a unique system was appearing high up on Dartmoor: the Haytor Granite Tramway. Opened in 1820, and operated until the 1850s, it was built by the landowner George Templer, who had contracts to supply granite for London Bridge and elsewhere. Extraordinarily, the tramway's so-called 'rails' were formed from the actual granite, with blocks cut to an average length of 5 ft (1 ft square in section, and with a 3 in deep rebate, 7 in from the inner edge, which formed a longitudinal flange for taking the plain metal wheels of the wagons). The gauge was about 4 ft 3 in. At junctions of branches and sidings, points were provided by additional grooves, a special device being inserted into a hole to guide wagons in the right direction.

The tramway was horse-drawn and descended 1300 ft from Haytor Down to the Stover Canal which connected with the Teign estuary. The distance from the quarry to the canal was 8 1/2 miles, but the tramway's total length was nearer 10 miles, with branches to various quarry faces. Much of the tramway (now scheduled as an ancient monument) can still be followed on the moor and also in places on the route down to Bovey Tracey. South from Bovey it became obliterated after being sold in 1862 by the then owner, the Duke of Somerset, to the Moretonhampstead & South Devon Railway Company (see pages 20-1).

Another horse-drawn tramway that transported granite and other goods was the Plymouth & Dartmoor Railway, constructed following Acts of 1819, 1820 and 1821. The 4 ft 6 in gauge single track line was opened as far as the King Tor quarries in 1823, and completed from Plymouth's Sutton Pool to Princetown in 1826. Direct distance covered was about 13 miles, but because of the topography and ascent of nearly 1400 ft the tortuous route measured 23 1/2 miles. The cast iron rails were laid in cast iron chairs to which they were bolted, although for cheapness some of the later rails were secured simply by large spikes being driven into the stone. Granite blocks supported the rails for most of the way.

The construction included a 620 yd tunnel at Leigham and sidings at quarries along the route, mostly laid with heavy granite blocks specially cut in the style of the metal rails for taking the wagons' wheels. In 1829 a short branch was added to serve Cann slate quarry near the River Plym. By 1840 traffic on the tramway had declined, although it continued until the 1860s. Later, the

Horse traction survived into the 20th century on the Lee Moor Tramway, here seen at Laira (Plymouth)

length above Yelverton was sold, reconstructed and reopened in 1883 as the Princetown Railway (see page 29). Remains of the earlier route can still be traced, particularly on Roborough Down.

Enterprises involving the chemical processing of Dartmoor peat prompted the use of tramways for bringing the material in from cutting areas to the works. One that existed briefly in these early years was in the Princetown area: a naphtha works was started at Bachelor's Hall in 1844, and moved into the then vacant prison two years later. Peat was cut at Greena Ball, Holming Beam and Fice's Well, and was transported along the tramway in metal trucks drawn by horses.

Another early peat tramway, dating from 1846, carried peat from cutting areas at Redlake to serve a naphtha works at Shipley Bridge, near South Brent. This, the Zeal Tor Tramway, comprised wooden rails bolted to granite blocks traversing Brent Moor, and horse-drawn trucks. The peat processing commenced in 1847, but again lasted only for a short period. Much of the track's route and some of the metal bolts can be traced.

So much for the earlier, quiet tramways. The time had come for the developing transport feature of the age to advance upon the Devon scene, bringing with it power, noise, and a new dimension to the lives of the county's people.

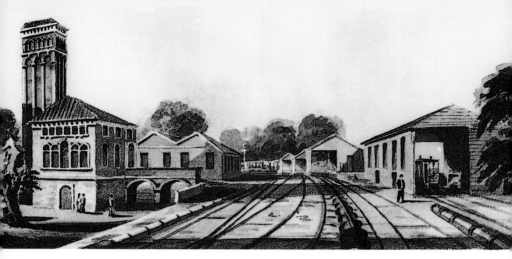

Newton Abbot Station in 1848, showing the 'atmospheric' pipes

The first main line

In the 1840s the Bristol & Exeter Railway began stretching out westwards in the form of an extension by the engineer Isambard Kingdom Brunel of the Great Western Railway (GWR) which had already been established from London Paddington to Bristol. By 1843 the 1092 yd brick-lined Whiteball tunnel beneath the Somerset–Devon boundary was under construction, and on 1 May 1844 the first train to travel the new line to Exeter burst from its western portal. Intermediate stations were provided at Tiverton Road, Cullompton, and Hele, others being added later. The line was of broad gauge, 7 ft 0 1/4 in, rather than the 'narrow' 4 ft 8 1/2 in, later known as the standard gauge.

Projection of the line to Plymouth, as the South Devon Railway, quickly followed. It was opened as far as Teignmouth in May 1846, and to Newton Abbot in the December. Although initially locomotives were worked on this stretch, their use – for a time – was made unnecessary because of an ingenious new method of propulsion: atmospheric power. The system involved a series of stationary engines connected to an iron pipe that was set between the rails. Along the top of the pipe ran a slot with

A Plymouth to Paddington steam special, passing Shaldon near Teignmouth in 1985

a flap cover which, when partially raised, enabled a rod from the train's leading carriage to connect with an elongated piston within the pipe. The vacuum created by the pumping engine, which caused a heavier air pressure behind the piston, provided the motive power.

By 1847 passengers were being conveyed by atmospheric propulsion to Teignmouth, and by 1848 to Newton Abbot. The system was swift, smooth, and relatively silent, but unfortunately problems arose, involving heavy maintenance costs – and the leather flaps were chewed by rats. In the autumn of 1848 the system was abandoned in favour of steam locomotives. A surviving atmospheric pumping station building can still be seen at Starcross, close to the railway.

The stretch of railway between Starcross and Teignmouth must be one of the most beautiful in the country, closely bordering the Exe estuary and the English Channel coast with its cliffs of red sandstone. However, five short tunnels, problems with the sea wall, and waves washing away ballast meant that construction was expensive. Even today the line sometimes requires urgent attention when encroached upon by exceptionally rough seas.

1848 also saw the opening of the continued line to Totnes

and Laira, Plymouth, as well as a branch from Newton Abbot to Torre (Torquay). The hilly country between Newton Abbot and Plymouth called for exacting construction measures. Steady inclines precede the Dainton and Marley tunnels (with a descent between them to Totnes and the crossing of the River Dart) and beyond to the 446 ft summit at Wrangaton. The River Erme valley at Ivybridge on the southern edge of Dartmoor, as well as that of the River Yealm and a tributary near Cornwood, had to be crossed by viaducts. The originals were made of timber, set on stone piers which stand close to the present replacement structures. There is a further incline at Hemerdon before Plymouth is reached.

In the same year a branch line was established farther east in the county, from the Bristol & Exeter Railway to Tiverton. Originally of broad gauge, construction of the 5 mile line called for a 40 ft aqueduct to carry the Grand Western Canal. Provision of this branch, following the main railway's advance, effectively shattered the hopes for an economic future for the canal and led to its demise.

Meanwhile, further developments were taking shape in and around Plymouth. From Laira the line was extended west and south (opened in 1849) to Millbay to serve the docks and packet ships. In 1853 a broad gauge line was opened from Laira to Sutton Harbour to supplement the earlier Plymouth & Dartmoor Railway. During the 1850s work continued the line westwards from Cornwall Junction, just north of Millbay, to the point where Brunel's bridge was being built high across the River Tamar to carry the railway on into Cornwall. The length of the line, which necessitated viaducts at Stonehouse Pool, Keyham and Weston Mill, and included the first station – Devonport – was opened to the public on 4 May 1859.

On the same day the impressive iron Royal Albert Bridge was inaugurated with due ceremony by the Prince Consort. Partially a suspension bridge with two main spans, it bore the broad gauge, single track line 100 ft above the Tamar which, at this point, is rather less than a quarter of a mile wide.

Also in 1859, on 22 June, a branch line to Tavistock was opened by the South Devon & Tavistock Railway Company. From a junction to the east of Plymouth, near Marsh Mills, the 13 mile single track railway ran through the difficult but beautiful terrain. There were stations at Bickleigh and Horrabridge (others were added later), tunnels at Shaugh, Yelverton and Grenofen, and six timber viaducts (later replaced with masonry) on stone piers.

Near the southern section of the line was the Lee Moor Tramway, which operated from 1858 until around 1940. It carried clay and bricks from the workings on Lee Moor to Plymouth's Cattewater quays. Power was provided by horses and cables until 1899 when locomotives were introduced on the upper section. The 4 ft 6 in gauge stretch of line leading to the Cattewater incorporated the lower section of the earlier Plymouth & Dartmoor Railway, and crossed the main line at Laira Junction. As successor to the P & D R, the tramway had the (horse-drawn) right of way over the main line, a right it officially continued to enjoy until 1961.

Another tramway was constructed to carry production from the rich copper mine, Devon Great Consols, on the east bank of the Tamar west of Tavistock, down to the river port of Morwellham. Brought into use in 1859 and worked until the 1890s, the 4 1/2 mile tramway was operated by locomotives and delivered material to the head of a double line inclined plane. Here the trucks were disconnected before descending two at a time on a rope, powered by a stationary engine sited at the top.

During the 1850s moves were made towards reaching north Devon by rail from Exeter. These were less attractive to investors than the more potentially profitable westward-pressing route, and projects became bogged down in protracted discussions and wranglings.

A first step forward was the establishment of the Exeter & Crediton Railway, for which an Act had been obtained in 1845.

Construction was delayed because of arguments between the proposed lessees – the Bristol & Exeter Railway and the London & South Western Railway Company (LSWR). The LSWR, as yet a somewhat remote force in Devon railways, was a shareholder in both the Exeter & Crediton and the proposed Taw Vale Extension – a horse-drawn tramway that operated from 1848 and connected Fremington with Barnstaple: it was proposed to convert it to a mechanised, narrow (standard) gauge railway.

The LSWR wanted the Crediton line also to be of standard gauge, while the Bristol & Exeter planned for broad. After deliberations, the Railway Commissioners decided that the Taw Vale Extension should be of broad gauge. This rather took the wind out of the LSWR's sails, and the company eventually withdrew in an apparent huff. Completion of the broad gauge line followed, from a junction at Cowley Bridge, a mile east of Exeter St David's, to Crediton. Leased as intended to the Bristol & Exeter, it was opened on 12 May 1851.

Early in 1852 the continuation of the line – the North Devon

Broad gauge train at Ivybridge, heading towards Newton Abbot

Bideford from the station – which was in East-the-Water, across the bridge from the old town. Stations could not always be located in town centres, and the effect was often to bring about development near the new railway

Railway – proceeded. The broad gauge route, mainly following the River Taw valley to Barnstaple, was opened in the summer of 1854. Construction of the Bideford Extension Railway followed, incorporating the section from Fremington relaid to broad gauge, and it was opened to Bideford for passengers on 2 November 1855.

The second main line

During the decade or so after its arrival Devon's first main railway line, comprising the Bristol & Exeter Railway and the South Devon Railway (which were to become part of the GWR in 1876) enjoyed increasing levels of traffic. Trade also built up on the early established branch lines and extensions.

Financial losses caused by the atmospheric fiasco were reversed as thousands of people, encouraged by excursion-rate fares and trains with many carriages, journeyed from London and elsewhere to experience the delights of the South-West.

By the late 1850s most of the original lines had been doubled, a notable exception being the North Devon Railway on which some sections, including the length between Copplestone and Umberleigh, always remained single.

For some time there had been calls for a second route from London to the South-West, on a more southerly line that avoided Bristol. From the 1840s the London & South Western Railway

The Devon Yeomanry disembarking from a train at Bideford. The Government favoured new railways as they made it easier to move troops and stores, particularly to Plymouth

was involved in railway schemes in Dorset and Somerset, and in Cornwall in 1846 it acquired the small Bodmin & Wadebridge Railway. Obviously the company was keen to extend its line to Exeter, and in fact plans already existed for it to do so.

In 1848 the LSWR obtained an Act for construction of a railway from Salisbury to Exeter, but because of difficulties in raising money and differences within the company, the plan was temporarily shelved. In the 1850s, however, the government needed better transport for naval and military forces along the south coastal areas, and was in favour of the route. A further Act was granted to the LSWR in 1856, in this case authorising a route to Exeter from Yeovil where there would be connection with the line from Salisbury. Work proceeded on the narrow gauge track, which was originally single (doubled in 1870). It entered Devon near Axminster from where the difficulties posed by the hilly terrain required skilful engineering solutions, including the 1353 yd Honiton tunnel. The railway, continuous now from Waterloo, was opened to Exeter on 19 July 1860.

Exeter's existing railway station at that time was the original St David's. Built for the arrival of the Bristol & Exeter Railway in 1844 and sited close to the River Exe, it was remote from the city centre and at a lower level. The LSWR provided its own station just below the level of Queen Street, by which name it became known.

Connection between the two stations and railway systems was desirable and so, following authorisation in 1860, work was carried out and the line opened on 1 February 1862. Construction of the 5/8 mile length involved making a tunnel and achieving a gradient of 1 in 37. LSWR trains could then continue through St David's Station eastwards to Cowley Bridge Junction and the connection with the Exeter & Crediton line.

Also in 1860 the LSWR took over the lease of the Exeter & Crediton from the Bristol & Exeter, and later, in 1862 and 1863 respectively, that of the Bideford Extension and the North Devon Railway. Their amalgamation with the LSWR followed in 1865.

Exeter St David's in 1953

Narrow gauge lines had been added to the broad gauge, from Exeter through to Bideford, to accommodate the LSWR's trains.

The layout at Exeter St David's meant that 'up' trains on the Bristol & Exeter's line and 'down' trains on the LSWR travelled in the same direction – the situation exists to this day and can be somewhat disconcerting when you're meeting a train from Salisbury which suddenly appears to be coming from the west!

With the arrival of the LSWR new prospects were brought to those living in the east of the county. Until the 1860s the area had been comparatively remote from a railway, its people being occupied mainly in farming, fishing, and lace-making. While towns such as Exmouth and Sidmouth were becoming known as genteel resorts for the privileged, seaside places west of the Exe were attracting greater numbers because of the South Devon Railway (SDR).

The ferry which operated between Exmouth and Starcross had only limited impact, and although in 1855 the Exeter & Exmouth Railway Company obtained powers for a broad gauge line to connect with the SDR at Exminster nothing came of it.

The railway was eventually laid some distance from the coastal towns and villages, a factor which undoubtedly helped preserve the area's quiet beauty and exclusiveness, but which did little to remedy depressions in the local economy.

The LSWR saw the need for an extension to Exmouth and, on establishing its line to Exeter, persuaded the Exeter & Exmouth company to construct a narrow gauge connecting line. This was opened on 1 May 1861, was subsequently worked by the LSWR and was absorbed by it in 1866. The railway prompted new developments, including building at Exmouth and docks that were opened in 1864.

Farther east, a branch was constructed by a private company southwards along the west bank of the River Axe, to what was then the village of Seaton. After it opened in 1868, Seaton developed into a small resort town, somewhat at the expense of the small ports of Axmouth and Beer on either side.

Leaving Colyford for Seaton Junction in 1954. 'Seaton Junction' was four miles north of Seaton, near Shute. It was closed in 1966 as part of the 'Beeching Plan'. Colyford Station survives as part of the Seaton & District Tramway, see pages 46-7

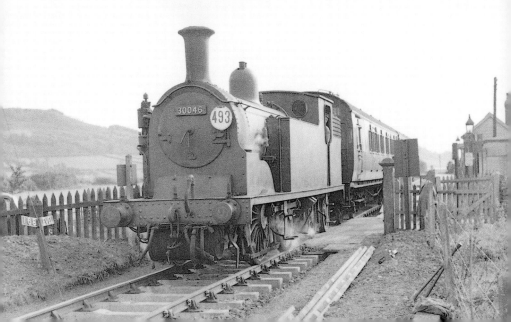

Reaching out

Following the establishment in 1844 and 1860 of the two main railway routes from London, there followed half a century or more of enthusiastic growth. Like trees rooted in fertile ground, the main trunks soon sprouted branches in all directions to reach most of the county's farther-flung districts. A notable exception was Hartland, the large parish on the north-west coastal extremity, which never acquired a railway connection. The nearest station was 13 miles distant at Bideford.

In general, more and more people were finding themselves within fairly easy reach of trains, with town and village stations and country halts giving access to local and national routes. Travel opened up new horizons for Devonians, while newcomers could savour the county's delights.

Devon had already witnessed the cutting and upheaval of its landscape by canal routes. Now it was the turn of rail engineers and their navvies to take over strips of the countryside as the new system quickly took shape. (Another innovative transport phenomenon – road and motorway developments – would impact on the county yet again and on an even greater scale during the twentieth century.)

Although the SDR had opened its branch from Newton Abbot to Torquay's Torre Station in 1848, services on the 5 mile line were limited. The need was seen for extension, to take in the shores of Torbay and connection with the mouth of the Dart. While Totnes at the head of the Dart's tidal waters had its station, Dartmouth remained remote from railways for a further sixteen years.

In 1857 proposals were made for a Dartmouth & Torbay Railway, the route presenting some difficulties due to the hilly coastline. The initial 3 miles to Paignton were opened in 1859, and the further 3 miles to Churston (then called Brixham Road) in 1861. More problems delayed the line's completion, largely because Dartmouth stands on the west side of the Dart estuary.

Steam at Goodrington on the Paignton & Dartmouth Railway in 1984. This line is today a justifiably popular tourist attraction

Termination at Kingswear, the small town on the east bank, was the decided solution, and the $3^1/4$ mile stretch, including the 495 yd Greenway tunnel, was opened on 16 August 1864. The ultimate connection with Dartmouth was made by steam ferry.

Dartmouth therefore had its railway station, but no rails. Connection from Churston to Brixham followed in 1868 with the opening of the 2 mile Torbay & Brixham Railway, a line much used for fish transport. Both the Dartmouth & Torbay and the Torbay & Brixham – each of broad gauge – were operated in their early years by the SDR. Encouraged by its increased traffic, the SDR meanwhile proceeded with doubling its broad gauge tracks. Between 1855 and 1861 conversion was completed on 30 miles of its routes, with 47 miles remaining single. By 1876 on the main line only the lengths between Dawlish and

Celebrating the arrival of the railway at Okehampton, 1871. For the first time people felt they were connected to the wider world

Teignmouth, and Rattery and Hemerdon, had not been doubled.

In 1862 negotiations took place between the newly incorporated Okehampton Railway Company (which changed its name in 1865 to the Devon & Cornwall – D & C), the LSWR, and the SDR. The issue under discussion was the Okehampton company's proposed narrow gauge railway westwards from the North Devon Railway at Coleford to Okehampton. An agreement was duly signed, but it precluded participation by the LSWR beyond Okehampton.

The Okehampton Railway, however, shortly obtained powers to extend its line to Lydford from where, with the prospect of an extra broad gauge rail to be laid by the forthcoming Launceston & South Devon Railway, it would enjoy a direct route to Plymouth via Tavistock.

With plans also afoot for railway extensions into Cornwall,

Bridestowe Station, immaculately maintained – as they all were. Notice the topiary trees and bushes!

the move caused chagrin to the LSWR. Anxious for reversal of the earlier terms, it sought further meetings, this time with the addition of the Bristol & Exeter company. The outcome of discussions was to the LSWR's advantage: the D&C was regarded as a subsidiary and in 1872 was absorbed by the major company.

Work on the line from Coleford Junction had been continuing since the mid-1860s: the stretch through Bow to North Tawton was opened in 1865 and the length to Okehampton Road (named Belstone Corner, and from 1872 Sampford Courtenay) in 1867; Okehampton town was reached on 3 October 1871. On the approach to Okehampton and beyond, the route climbed around the northern slopes of Dartmoor. The continuation to Lydford, opened in 1874, included an ascent to 950 ft at Meldon – the highest point on the LSWR and later Southern Railway – with a spectacular iron viaduct of girder spans. It was supported by five latticed piers and carried the line 120ft above the West Okement valley.

During the subsequent descent to Lydford the nine-arched stone Sourton viaduct gave passengers a dramatic glimpse of valley slopes and a sense of the remoteness of the nearby moor. Initially single, the line was fully doubled, including additions to the Meldon viaduct's structure, by 1879. (For modern use see page 46.)

Launceston, just over the border in Cornwall, had previously pressed for a railway connection to Plymouth. This took shape as the Launceston & South Devon Railway, a subsidiary of the SDR authorised by an Act in 1862. From the railhead at Tavistock the line took a roughly northward course, leaving the Tavy valley to join that of the River Burn, with a halt for Mary Tavy & Blackdown before Lydford. From Lydford Station it then swung westward, following the River Lyd valley, with a halt at Liddaton and stations at Coryton and Lifton, and eventually running close to the upper Tamar which it crossed in leaving the county.

Comprising 19 miles, the line was completed and opened in 1865. Its establishment was of interest to the LSWR on its arrival at Lydford in 1874. By laying an agreed third rail within the broad gauge, from 1876 the LSWR could share the Tavistock & Launceston Railway line from Lydford to Marsh Mills, Plymouth, continuing by the same means on the main line through to Devonport.

In the 1860s another line, in the south of the county, brought the railway system within reach of Dartmoor. In 1858 the Newton & Moretonhampstead Railway Company (reconstituted in 1861 as the Moretonhampstead & South Devon Railway Company, chaired by the Earl of Devon) had been incorporated and a survey made for a line from the SDR at Newton Abbot to Bovey Tracey, Lustleigh and Moretonhampstead.

The proposed route was to run through the grounds of the Stover estate, so negotiations with its owner, the Duke of Somerset, took place. At this time the duke also owned the

Stover Canal and the Haytor Granite Tramway which connected with the canal but had recently become disused.

Seeing the opportunity for a deal, the duke persuaded the railway company to purchase both the canal and the tramway as far as Bovey Tracey. The sale, for £8000, was completed on the condition that the company construct and maintain a siding at Bovey for possible granite use.

Building of the 12 1/4 miles of broad gauge proceeded, and the railway was opened on 4 July 1866. Following the route of the earlier Haytor Tramway as far as Bovey, it rose in altitude over its entire length from 50 ft to 588 ft. To comply with specifications, it was built with bridges wide enough for double rails, but in fact it always remained single. Costs escalated during construction and the company faced financial problems before completion, succeeding only with difficulty in raising the extra sum. Absorbed by the SDR in 1872, the line brought many people into the area for moorland holidays besides carrying commercial traffic.

Back in Exeter, where St David's Station was enlarged, improved and re-opened in 1864, a short branch from the SDR to the City Basin of the Exeter Canal was brought into use in 1867. Constructed to carry both broad and narrow gauge traffic, the branch left the SDR about half a mile out of St David's (a third rail was laid on this length of down line) and then ran north for approximately the same distance to the Basin.

The 1870s saw a proliferation of railway developments in Devon. A line from the SDR to Ashburton had been in prospect from the early 1860s, and this was given powers with the incorporation of the Buckfastleigh, Totnes & South Devon Railway in 1864, with the addition of Ashburton in 1865. Local people had to wait until 1 May 1872 before the 7 mile railway from Totnes to Buckfastleigh and a further 2 3/4 miles to Ashburton were opened, but they made the most of the occasion with special festivities in the nearby Station Meadow. (My grandfather, as a boy, was given a day's leave from boarding school to travel on the train for the inauguration, and my grandmother remembered that the day was extremely hot.)

Buckfastleigh was a busy station, with the wool trade providing much outward traffic and coal being brought in. The line runs through very beautiful rural countryside, closely following the River Dart for most of the way. (For modern developments see pages 45-6.)

At Totnes a branch of about ³/₄ mile from the station to the town's quay on the Dart, known as Totnes Quay Branch, was opened in 1873. It was worked mainly by horses, but locomotives were used latterly, traversing the main street leading to the bridge and the Paignton road by a level crossing.

For some time ideas had existed for a railway to connect with the Bristol & Exeter line at Norton Fitzwarren, just west of Taunton, and to run on through west Somerset and across north Devon to Barnstaple. Although an Act for the Devon & Somerset Railway was obtained in 1864, work was protracted. Financial problems largely intervened, and resulted in unwelcome economies being made, causing hunger to navvies and a low standard

Ilfracombe Station, March 1908

of station construction. Gradually progress was made and at last the 43 mile line was fully opened to Barnstaple on 1 November 1873: the new station was on the east side of the town and was later identified as Victoria Road.

Passing close to the foothills of Exmoor the line went through some wild and dramatic scenery, crossing the River Bray at Filleigh on a high viaduct. It ran north of Bampton, south of Dulverton (which had its station 2 miles from the town) and north of South Molton, where again the station was at a little distance. People from the small towns and villages on the route soon took advantage of the facility for getting to the bigger towns, and eventually the line carried agricultural produce and machinery, and coal. Of broad gauge, single track, the line was leased to the Bristol & Exeter Railway Company.

Ilfracombe, a small Bristol Channel port on the north Devon coast with prospects of becoming a resort, was also seeking railway connection during the early 1860s. The Devon & Somerset was unable, in its pecuniary state, to fulfil an agreement for a joint line, so one was sought instead with the LSWR which already had a station at Barnstaple. Consequently an Act for the Barnstaple & Ilfracombe Railway, as a subsidiary of the LSWR, was passed in 1870.

The 16 mile line was difficult to build, requiring a metal bridge across the River Taw downstream of Barnstaple's ancient bridge, and then, after a relatively level stretch along the east bank of the estuary, ascending and descending gradients and sharp curves. The route, which included a station at Braunton and one for Mortehoe, was opened on 20 July 1874.

While the Ilfracombe railway made possible a direct route from Exeter to the seaside town and points between, the Devon & Somerset did not miss out entirely, as in 1873 it instituted a horse-drawn coach service from its Barnstaple terminus to Ilfracombe. Despite objections by the LSWR, the service continued until 1887, when a 1 mile loop was opened to connect the two stations.

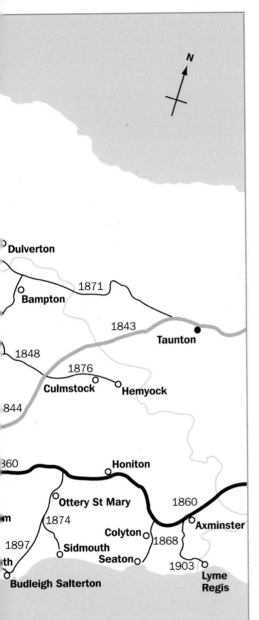

The development of Devon's railways

As the main text of this book shows, much of the railway system was put together piecemeal, with a number of companies responding to the opportunities which presented themselves.

But by 1900, a pattern had emerged. The GWR and LSWR had been thinking strategically and each now had a main line to both Exeter and Plymouth, with branch connections in their own sphere of influence.

Key

━━━ *GWR main line*
━━━ *LSWR main line*
──── *branch lines*

The dates shown indicate when the lines opened

By now, Torrington was also on the LSWR system: an extension from Bideford had been opened on 18 July 1872.

East Devon saw some further developments too in the 1870s. Sidmouth had so far remained aloof from the railway system, despite earlier abortive plans to establish a harbour and a rail link to it. But now, as the town grew, rail ideas were revived. The $8\frac{1}{2}$ mile, single track Sidmouth Railway branched from the LSWR at Sidmouth Junction and followed the west bank of the River Otter southwards, with stations at Ottery St Mary and Tipton St John's. It then swung south-eastwards for the final run towards Sidmouth. It was opened on 6 July 1874.

Optimistically embarked upon by local people, the Culm Valley Railway – a 'Light Railway' (these were built economically for areas with small numbers of inhabitants) – provided a connection eastwards from the main line at Tiverton Junction through rich farm land to the large villages of Uffculme, Culmstock and Hemyock. The $7\frac{1}{2}$ mile line, for which powers had been granted in 1873, was opened on 29 May 1876. However, traffic did not come up to expectations, and the owners sold the line in 1880 to the GWR. Apart from passengers, it was much used for

An early wooden viaduct at Torrington

goods, serving the woollen mill at Uffculme and the large dairy at Hemyock.

Also connected with the Bristol & Exeter Railway, a little farther north, was a tramway carrying material from the large limestone quarry at Westleigh. Originally of 3 ft gauge but later converted to standard, and approximately a mile in length, it left the quarry through a tunnel under the road and was carried on an embankment south-eastwards towards the Grand Western Canal. Here the line branched, one section going northwards to a wharf at Fossend, and the other crossing the canal on a small viaduct to terminate at Burlescombe Station.

Major company changes occurred in 1876 which saw the demise of both the Bristol & Exeter Railway and the South Devon Railway, and their passing to the more powerful GWR.

Other events were taking place at this time on the LSWR's route beyond Okehampton. Back in 1865, when the Okehampton Railway changed its name to the Devon & Cornwall, powers were obtained for an extension to Bude in Cornwall, as well as to Torrington. These powers, however, had now lapsed, but it was suggested that a single line be constructed from Meldon Junction as far as Holsworthy. This was authorised in 1873 and opened on 20 January 1879. Running north-westwards and west, the 19 mile line passed through some of the county's most thinly populated areas. Roughly half-way was Halwill (later Halwill Junction) which for many years served as a centre for agricultural goods.

At first the arrival of the railway at Holsworthy provided a boost to trade in sea sand from the town's terminus of the Bude Canal, but very soon the canal's trade declined, leading ultimately to its closure.

The construction at Holsworthy included a stone-built eight-arch viaduct, just east of the town. (An extension to Bude was eventually opened in 1898, including an impressive nine-arched 50 ft high concrete viaduct west of Holsworthy, at Derriton, which has been restored as a cycle route.)

A typical scene at Halwill Junction, a centre for agricultural goods

About 4 miles south from Meldon Junction the Rattlebrook Peat Railway in 1879 met the main line with a siding at Bridestowe Station. This 5 mile, 4 ft 8 1/2 in gauge railway served the Rattlebrook Peatworks high on the moor. At first horse-drawn but later mechanised, it followed a steep and tortuous route to accomplish an ascent from 800 ft at Bridestowe to 1750 ft at the peatworks in the boggy area between Great Links Tor and Amicombe Hill. A crossing of the Okehampton–Tavistock road was made just beyond Bridestowe Station, and the route included a reversing length to enable a change of direction. The rails were removed in 1931 after which motor vehicles were used for some years.

On the other side of Dartmoor, the Teign Valley Railway was under construction in the early 1880s. The narrow-gauge, 7 mile single track ran from Heathfield, north of Newton Abbot on the Moretonhampstead line, north-eastwards to Chudleigh, and then north through the valley of the River Teign to Ashton. It was opened on 9 October 1882 and worked by the GWR. Although continuation to Exeter was shortly projected, some time elapsed before this actually happened.

An accident at Halwill Junction, 3 July 1905

Back across the moor again, the company running the horse-drawn Plymouth & Dartmoor Railway had long been beset with many problems, and traffic had dwindled. The upper section, from Yelverton to Princetown, was sold to a private company, reconstructed with some deviations, and opened as the Princetown Railway on 11 August 1883. Of 4 ft 8½ in gauge, the line was managed by the GWR until taken over by it in 1921.

Connection with the Plymouth–Tavistock line had originally to be made at Horrabridge, but in 1885 a station was provided at Yelverton. The 10½ mile route to Princetown was of high scenic quality, but subject to severe conditions in winter. After Dousland and Burrator Halt it passed high beside Burrator Reservoir before ascending over the open moorland in wide loops. There was an isolated halt at Ingra Tor, and others, with sidings, to serve the Swell Tor, King Tor and Foggintor granite quarries. The station at Princetown, at an altitude of 1373 ft, was the highest on the GWR.

Inland links between railways featured particularly in the mid-1880s. The Exe Valley branch provided a connection between the GWR's main route to Exeter and the line through north Devon to Barnstaple. Although Tiverton had its branch from the Bristol & Exeter Railway from 1848, the town was growing and increased facilities were desirable. The Tiverton & North Devon Railway, from Tiverton to a junction at Morebath, had been authorised in 1875; eventually the 10 mile line was built and opened on 1 August 1884, with trains continuing on the Barnstaple line the further 2 miles to Dulverton.

The Exe Valley Railway was authorised in 1874, with powers handed to the Bristol & Exeter the following year. Connecting Tiverton with Stoke Canon on the main line, a distance of 11 miles with a further 4 on to Exeter, the railway was built by the GWR and opened on 1 May 1885. Both lines were originally termed 'narrow', but were now becoming known as 'standard'. Passengers could enjoy the delights of the valley scenery. From Tiverton through to West Exe Halt, Cadeleigh, Burn Halt, Up Exe, Thorverton and Brampford Speke, and again after Stoke Canon, the line ran close by the River Exe, amid green hills and meadows. Similarly the line north also followed the river, with stops at Bolham Halt, Cove, and Bampton, before taking the Batherm valley for Morebath Junction.

Another link was between Halwill and Launceston: the first stage of the North Cornwall Railway was constructed by the LSWR and opened on 21 July 1892. The 15 mile line joined the River Carey valley on its south-westerly route, with stations at Ashwater and Tower Hill (for St Giles-on-the-Heath).

Two notable developments in the history of Devon's railways took place in the early 1890s. The first was the establishment of a second route to the Plymouth area, for which there had been pressure by the LSWR for some time. Owned by the Plymouth, Devonport & South Western Junction Railway Company, the line was worked from its opening on 2 June 1890 by the LSWR. The 22½ mile narrow, double track extended south from

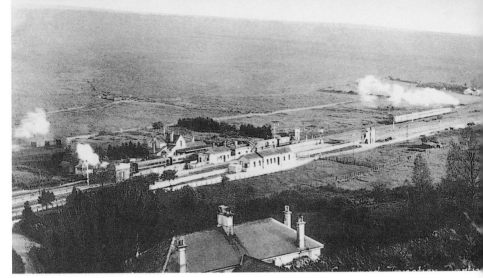

Lydford, where the LSWR and GWR stations stood side by side, seen from Was Tor c.1910. Very little now remains

Lydford and kept company with the Launceston branch line through a new Brentor Station as far as Mary Tavy (whose station the LSWR now ceased to serve). It then curved westwards, crossing the older line, to a new Tavistock (later 'north') station.

Beyond Tavistock the line headed for the Tamar valley, with stations at this stage at Bere Alston and Bere Ferrers and, in the Plymouth environs, St Budeaux, Ford, Devonport and North Road, before terminating at a new one at Friary. A station was opened at Tamerton Foliot in 1898, and halts at Weston Mill, Camel's Head and Albert Road in 1906.

The construction included many impressive features, including: Shillamill tunnel just south of Tavistock; two tunnels under Devonport; the Wallabrook, Tavistock and Shillamill viaducts in the Tavistock area; Ford viaduct at Plymouth; and two metal viaducts over water – the girder Tavy viaduct over the Tavy's mouth into the Tamar, and the Ernesettle viaduct over Tamerton Lake. There were also many bridges along the route.

The line offered a new means of transport for produce from the Tamar Valley's market garden industry and, after development of the Stonehouse Pool Branch passenger ocean terminal

This was taken at Teignmouth just before the conversion to standard gauge in May 1892: additional shorter sleepers have been inserted as a prelude to the frantic weekend's work

in 1904, competition with the GWR in speed to London.

The second development concerned the standardisation of gauge. For some years narrow gauge trains could run on sections of the former Bristol & Exeter's broad (7 ft 0 1/2 in) gauge lines by means of a third rail within the track. However, by the mid-1870s, many miles of the system in Somerset had been converted to the 4 ft 8 1/2 in gauge, and by the 1880s Devon's lengths of surviving broad gauge, although liked by travellers for their comfort, were deteriorating. Conversion had been under consideration in 1875 as part of negotiations for takeover by the GWR, and in subsequent years the surviving mixture became increasingly inconvenient. Total conversion, from purely broad to narrow, was eventually agreed on, and the work was carried out during the weekend of 20-23 May 1892. Removal of the third rail from mixed lines followed. By now the former 'narrow' gauge was known as 'standard'.

During the busy railway years numerous small lines were added in the area of Plymouth, Stonehouse and Devonport. They comprised sidings, spurs, loop and connection lines, and small branches to serve quays, docks and the Dockyard.

The 1890s also saw completion of a new GWR branch to Kingsbridge (an unsuccessful scheme was started, but never finished, in the 1860s). Opened on 19 December 1893, the 14 mile route branched from the main line at Brent and ran southwards along the Avon valley, with stations at Avonwick, Gara Bridge and Loddiswell. Farther east, the Budleigh Salterton Railway was added to the scene, leaving Tipton St John's on the Sidmouth branch and continuing for 7 miles down the Otter valley to the small coastal resort. There were intermediate stations at Newton Poppleford and Otterton. Opened on 15 May 1897, the line was taken over in 1912 by the LSWR, which had already extended it a further 4 miles west to Exmouth in 1903.

Another branch from Plymouth, built by the GWR, was the Yealmpton Branch, opened on 17 January 1898. Approximately 9 miles in length, it ran from Millbay Station and along the route had stations at Billacombe, Elburton, Brixton and Steer Point.

A busy scene at Brent, with a horse special about to load. The passenger train has just arrived from Kingsbridge

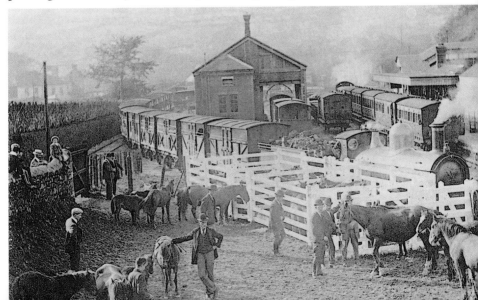

The 'Yeo', one of the locomotives of the much loved Lynton &
Barnstaple Railway, with railway staff

Two interesting railways associated with the north Devon coast came into existence around the turn of the century. The Lynton & Barnstaple Railway was the inspiration of a small local company whose members included the publisher and local benefactor Sir George Newnes. The plan was to open up the remote, dramatic coastline on Exmoor's fringe, and a railway of true narrow gauge (1 ft 11 1/2 in) was agreed.

It was opened on 16 May 1898. Because of the steep slopes and high altitudes of the intervening hills, both construction and maintenance proved far more costly than expected. Starting at Barnstaple, the 19 mile line had stations at Chelfham, Bratton Fleming, Blackmoor Gate, Woody Bay and Lynton, with halts at Snapper, Parracombe and Caffyns. There was also a 390 ft long, 72 ft high, eight-arched white brick viaduct across the Stoke Rivers valley at Chelfham. The railway's life was relatively short: it was bought by the Southern Railway in the 1920s, and by 1935

Pilton Station (Barnstaple), with the sheds of the narrow gauge Lynton & Barnstaple Railway

(19 September) it had closed due to dwindling passenger numbers – travel by road was becoming preferable. Today enthusiasts have embarked upon its restoration (see page 47).

The second small railway in north Devon, the Bideford, Westward Ho! & Appledore Railway, had an even shorter life. Successor to an earlier, more grandiose but abortive scheme empowered in 1866, it was authorised in 1896 and opened on 20 May 1901. The light railway took a route west from Bideford Quay to Abbotsham cliffs and then followed the coast north-eastwards to Northam, a distance of 5 miles. The 1¹/₂ mile extension to Appledore was opened on 1 May 1908.

Trains would stop by request at recognised halts, and there were stations at Westward Ho! and Appledore. However, the First World War brought the railway's demise when its track and locomotives were requisitioned by the government, and it closed on 17 March 1917. Temporary rails were laid across Bideford

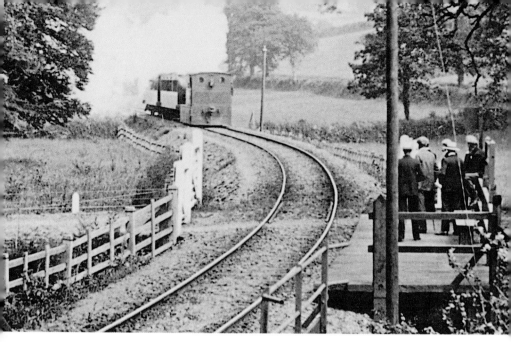

*Waiting for the train at Kenwith Halt on the Bideford,
Westward Ho! & Appledore Railway*

Bridge on Sunday 29 July the same year to enable the departing locomotives to travel over to the LSWR.

A few more railway developments were yet to be introduced to Devon in the early twentieth century. The Exeter Railway involved linking Exeter with the Teign Valley line, which effectively provided an alternative to the main line between Exeter and Newton Abbot. Although authorised in 1883, it was not opened until 1 July 1903. Extending from the existing Teign line at Ashton, the route continued northwards up the valley, with stations at Doddiscombsleigh and Dunsford, and then east with further stations at Longdown and Ide and a halt at Alphington before Exeter's St Thomas Station. Worked by the GWR, the 11 mile line included two tunnels – one just before and one after Longdown Station.

The Tamar Valley Railway in west Devon had its origins in 1891 when the Plymouth, Devonport & South Western Junction Railway took over the 3 ft 6 in gauge East Cornwall Mineral

Calstock Viaduct under construction in July 1906, still in use on the Gunnislake–Plymouth branch line

Railway. This originally started from Calstock Quay and, after conversion to standard gauge, went across the River Tamar into Devon by a new 129 ft high viaduct at Calstock. Joining the main line at Bere Alston, the new work became part of the Callington Branch and gave the Cornish town and Gunnislake improved rail communications into Plymouth and beyond. It was also a valued means of transport for Tamar Valley growers as well as for ordinary passengers.

A very short length of standard gauge railway, the Mamhead Military, existed during the First World War. It led from the goods yard at Starcross Station on the GWR main line to woods behind the village and carried timber cut by prisoners of war.

The last new line in the history of Devon's railways was that of the North Devon & Cornwall Junction Light Railway. This mainly remote route provided a connection between Torrington and Halwill over a distance of 22 miles and served the ball clay working areas at Petersmarland and Meeth. The northern

An Adams 460 Class 4-4-0 at Hatherleigh Station

6 miles from Torrington replaced an earlier 3ft tramway. Along the standard gauge route, which was opened on 27 July 1925, were a number of halts: the first was at Watergate and there were others near Petersmarland, Meeth, Hatherleigh and Highampton before arrival at Halwill Junction.

In a different category, but worthy of note, two cliff railways were established in Devon. The first, from Lynton to Lynmouth, dates from 1890; the second, at Babbacombe (Torquay), from 1926. Both still survive.

The end of the LSWR came in 1923 when the company became part of the Southern Railway, one of four large independent British railway companies that dominated the scene until nationalisation in 1948.

Retraction

By the turn of the nineteenth to the twentieth century Devon's railway system was almost fully in place and reaching the peak of its success. In less than sixty years the county had acquired a swift means of transport with countrywide connections, bringing lines of communication and new prospects within reach of most people, even in remote areas.

Rail travel became fashionable, and traffic of both passengers and goods grew, particularly during the two World Wars.

In many places the Devon countryside had taken on a new appearance. In essentially quiet pastural places, or in previously remote river valleys, one might come across a fenced linear intrusion of well-maintained stone ballast, wood sleepers and metal rails, indicating that here was a route of some significance. Then, possibly, a distant rhythmic rumble would be heard, becoming gradually louder. A train was coming. Presently it appeared, perhaps approaching a nearby bridge from which it would then speedily emerge in all glory, passing by with whistle sounding, and soon disappearing down the track with a puffing and hissing that left a cloud of steam in its wake as the sound died away.

Station staff took great pride in their work

The Cornish Riviera Express, passing opposite Shaldon in 1959,
a brand new 'Warship' heralding the dawn of the diesel age

Like the lengths of railway, stations – many of which incorporated a goods yard – were usually well-kept. Platforms were swept, waiting rooms often had a fire in winter. Uniforms were worn by staff who, in many cases, used time between trains to create colourful flower beds, sometimes with the station name picked out in whitened stones, which enhanced the scene.

The trains, too, despite tending to blacken from the effects of smoke and smuts, were smart in their distinctive livery. The GWR reverted to its traditional 'chocolate and cream' carriages in 1923; the LSWR livery was of brown and salmon colours, while green was favoured by the succeeding SR.

Early carriages had 'through' compartments, but corridor trains became standard use for many years on main routes. Branch lines often had 'open plan' systems, with some seats arranged similarly to those of modern carriages (minus the tables) while others were fixed with their backs to windows.

Carriage partitions bore monochrome photographs of distant attractions, such as Cheltenham Spa, the Wye Valley, or the Menai Bridge, to tempt travellers farther, while stations were often adorned with colourful posters for places like Newquay, showing an azure sea and constantly shining sun.

During the 1920s and 30s road travel developed considerably and in the late 1940s was making major new advances. Rail transport in contrast began to falter. Following election of the Labour government in 1945 the railways were nationalised in 1948 as British Railways (later changed to British Rail).

In 1963 a scientist and director of ICI, Dr Richard (later Lord) Beeching, was appointed chairman of the British Railways Board and in the same year he presented to Parliament a report which sparked much controversy. It embodied plans to concentrate on inter-city passenger traffic and to centralise goods depots, which foreshadowed huge closures.

Even before the report, however, branch line closures had already begun in Devon. Apart from the Yealmpton Branch which, following its early closing in 1930, had reopened from 1941-7 for the benefit of people who had moved out from wartime Plymouth, the first casualty was the passenger service on the Turnchapel Branch. This closed on 10 September 1951.

The Princetown Railway was closed on 5 March 1956 and the 1950s also signalled the end of the Teign Valley line between Exeter and Heathfield. The section from Exeter to Christow closed on 9 June 1958, although dwindling freight traffic still operated on the southern sections until 1965. The Dart Valley line from Totnes to Buckfastleigh and Ashburton closed to passengers on 5 November 1958 and to goods on 10 September 1962. For this line, however, there was to be a new future (see pages 45-6). The Moretonhampstead Branch, whose use had lessened ever since the war, faced a similar fate: the line was closed to passengers on 2 March 1959, freight traffic continuing until the section above Bovey Tracey was closed on 6 April 1964 and that between Heathfield and Bovey in 1970.

The line of the Princetown Railway, now a foot and cycle path which winds its way sinuously across Dartmoor

During the 1960s railway closures proliferated in what could be described as a decade of decline. In all directions services were reduced, halts and stations closed, and routes discontinued. Often, it seemed to many people, schedules were made inconvenient to discourage rail use, and thus to provide a case for withdrawal.

The former GWR main line through Devon, and branches from it, soon became subject to the cuts. Although stations west of Exeter (except Exminster) as far as Totnes remained open, between Totnes and Plymouth they were all closed on 2 March 1959 – except for Brent, which survived until 5 October 1964 (the branch from Brent to Kingsbridge closed on 16 September 1963). The line from Plymouth through Tavistock South, to Lydford and Launceston, was axed for passenger use from 31 December 1962, although goods traffic continued on some sections until 1966.

East of Exeter, all Devon stations on the line, except Tiverton Junction, closed on 5 October 1964. The branch from the Junction to Tiverton closed to passengers on the same day and for freight on 5 June 1967. The Culm Valley line from Tiverton

Junction had already closed to passengers on 9 September 1963, although Hemyock's dairy traffic caused limited line reprieve until 1975. Tiverton had already seen the last of its Exe Valley trains: the line from Stoke Canon through to Morebath Junction ended its days on 7 October 1963, although carriage of grain from Stoke Canon to Thorverton continued until 1966. The line from Taunton to Barnstaple closed completely on 3 October 1966.

The former Southern route also suffered. The train service was down-graded in September 1964, two years later most of the intermediate stations were closed, and the final ignominy was the singling of the line in 1967.

With many main line services being withdrawn, passenger numbers fell and routes west of Exeter and around Plymouth were soon curtailed. The line from Okehampton via Meldon Junction to Halwill and those on to Holsworthy and Launceston closed on 3 October 1966. The one from Okehampton through Tavistock to Bere Alston closed from 6 May 1968, and the Exeter to Okehampton on 5 June 1972, although the latter has retained its rails and carries occasional trains.

It is hardly surprising, then, that by the 1970s Devon's railways were considerably reduced. The North Devon line still existed, but the passenger service from Barnstaple to Torrington had ceased on 4 October 1965 (transport of milk and clay continued until 1982) and the line to Ilfracombe closed on 5 October 1970. Barnstaple's three stations were reduced to just one, the former Junction, and the service became but a shadow of earlier days when the Atlantic Coast Express regularly swept along the rails.

In south Devon British Railways services on the Torbay line were discontinued beyond Paignton in 1973, the line from Brixham having been closed on 13 May 1963 – however, the length from Paignton to Kingswear is another that enjoys a new life (see pages 46-7).

The last notable closure was to the line from Torrington to Halwill. Passenger services had ended previously on 1 March

The last day at Lifton, on the GWR branch from Plymouth to Launceston. Closure of this line in December 1962 was delayed by a great snowstorm, which trapped two of the trains

1965, but the line from Meeth to Torrington and on to Barnstaple continued for clay traffic. Eventual official closure was on 8 November 1982.

And so the face of Devon had changed again.

Even the locomotives became radically different, with diesel engines appearing from 1958 and replacing steam on the main lines by 1964. Many Devonians living in remote areas of the county were more isolated than they could remember. For example, an inhabitant of Morebath, a village near Exmoor, could until 1965 travel easily to towns such as South Molton or Barnstaple in one direction, to Taunton in another, or south to Tiverton or Exeter. That was now very much a thing of the past. 'So much for progress' was the observation of many.

The later scene

In 1994, under a Conservative government, privatisation returned: on 1 April Railtrack was created and its successor Network Rail now owns almost the entire rail infrastructure in Devon. The various train companies are charged for access. These comprise: Southwest Trains, running a service on the former SR main line from Waterloo to Exeter; Great Western Trains, operating the Intercity service from Paddington; Virgin Cross Country, providing the Intercity service from other areas; and Wales & West which runs surviving branch lines and main line stopping services. Rail Express System operates mail trains, and English Welsh & Scottish (EWS) provides freight services. High Speed Trains – known as Intercity 125s – were introduced in 1979 and are now used on most long distance routes.

The chief surviving railway route through early twenty-first century Devon is that of the former GWR main line – successor

In summer, steam trains run between Buckfastleigh and Totnes

Trams, constructed at two-thirds scale, today run on the former line from Colyton to Seaton

to the Bristol & Exeter and the SDR. It connects from Paddington and the north with Exeter, Newton Abbot and the branch to Torquay and Paignton, and with Plymouth, and it continues along the length of Cornwall.

The former Southern (previously LSWR) main line from Waterloo ends at Exeter, but connects with the branch to Exmouth. Both serve several stations and service also continues on the north Devon line (now called the Tarka Line) from Exeter St David's to Barnstaple. And the line from Yeoford Junction to Meldon beyond Okehampton now ends at Okehampton, following closure of Meldon quarry. West Devon, too, still has its Tamar Valley line into Plymouth.

In addition there has been some restoration of lines. After its closure, the Totnes–Buckfastleigh line was bought by the Dart Valley Light Railway Company and has been developed as a tourist attraction. During the summer season steam trains are operated, the line being leased by the South Devon Railway Trust from the Dart Valley Company which also runs steam trains on the Paignton & Dartmouth Railway from Paignton to Kingswear. In east Devon 3 miles of the railway from Seaton to Colyton are in use as the Seaton Tramway, on which passenger trams run alongside the River Axe. Work is also being carried out to restore sections of the former Lynton & Barnstaple line in north Devon for interest and tourist attraction. Initially a distance of 1 mile of the narrow gauge line has been completed and reopened, giving visitors a 'there-and-back' trip. All of the line as well as the former stations are owned by the company, which intends to proceed over time.

The Plym Valley Railway is a recently developed heritage railway based on $1^1/_2$ miles of the former South Devon & Tavistock Railway route near Plymouth northward from Marsh Mills (see page 9). Here a centre has been formed for preserving steam and diesel and other railway artifacts. At the Devon Railway Centre at Bickleigh near Tiverton a half mile stretch of the Exe Valley track has been restored and carries a small steam driven train for visitors, while the old Moretonhampstead Railway is usable from Newton Abbot to Heathfield.

Instow signal box, a feature of the Tarka Trail

After closures in the 1960s and 70s rail lines were offered to local authorities, but were declined, and so most were sold to adjacent landowners. Consequently, some routes are now used as accommodation farm tracks, while others have reverted to natural habitats. Yet others have been built over or converted by local authorities into modern roads. A few have benefited from the boom in leisure activities and been converted by local authorities to walking and cycling routes. A notable example is the 'Tarka Trail' from Barnstaple through Bideford and Torrington to Petrockstowe. Walking and cycling are now well established along the former Plymouth-Tavistock route.

Ever increasing road use, notably by heavy vehicles and by commuters to Exeter and Plymouth, plus the region's important holiday industry, have led to pressures towards restoring the former westward rail route around the north of Dartmoor. The need is underlined by problems that can occur in some seasons due to stormy seas and high tides which can invade the coast around Dawlish and necessitate closure of the railway line, thus disconnecting Plymouth and Cornwall from the system. Much rejoicing accompanied the eventual decision to restore regular service between Exeter St David's and Okehampton. The line had still been usable but new track and sleepers and other works were needed. The Dartmoor Line as it is called was reopened in partnership between the GWR and Devon County Council in November 2021. It joins the line to Barnstaple at Coleford Junction. Okehampton Station has been improved and further works are planned, and a Parkway station proposed for commuter convenience.

To gain full connection of the round-the-moor route, restoration of the connections east and west of Tavistock would be required, and there are strong hopes that this can be achieved. The route still exists although the tracks are gone, and the present spectacular Meldon viaduct would need to be replaced with a stronger one for the heavier trains..The Tamar Valley line still has its station and regular service into Plymouth. Hopes are high.